THE GIFT OF REST

THE GIFT OF REST

Christy,
Thank you so much for
leading us in worship of our
Savior at our Christmas Dinner
this year! We are so thankful
for you!
A pray God will use this Bible
Study to guide you into sweet
rest. In His love, Crickett

Crickett Keeth

CROSSLINK
PUBLISHING

The Gift of Rest

 CrossLink Publishing
www.crosslinkpublishing.com

ISBN 978-1-63357-040-5

Library of Congress Control Number: 2015945867

"Rest is like the handle on a mug: the empty space is what makes it useful. And Crickett Keeth knows how much we need those empty spaces in our lives. Her Bible studies have long been my favorites, with their emphasis on digging into the text and applying it where readers live. And her study on rest is no exception. In this study readers encounter the Sabbath-making God who calls followers to rest, reflect, and find rejuvenation in contrast to our crazy, fast-paced, get-identity-from-doing-stuff world."

—Dr. Sandra Glahn, author of the Coffee Cup Bible Study series, seminary professor

In our hurried, hectic, iPhone world, many of us are desperately in need of rest. We know it, yet we continue to run through life at break-neck speed resulting in physical, emotional, and spiritual exhaustion, burn out, and stressed relationships. What will it take to slow us down? Crickett Keeth's The Gift of Rest thoroughly explores the varied aspects of God's mandated rest in an eight-week, discovery-style, application-oriented Bible study. This study will persuade women to reject today's typical destructive life pace and trade it in for a productive, healthy, all-in, Christ-centered lifestyle instead. Consider the difference that could make!!!

—Dr. Sue Edwards, Author of The Discover Together Bible Study Series and co-author of Organic Mentoring; Associate Professor of Educational Ministries and Leadership, Dallas Theological Seminary

"This is the kind of study I look for as a small-group leader. The Gift of Rest presents sound doctrine in a user-friendly format that enriched my personal understanding of resting in the Father's love. I look forward to using it in our group to discuss the Bible-based connections Crickett draws between rest, contentment, trust, and peace."

—Jim Davis, author of Why Me? (And Why that's the Wrong Question)

"In a frenetic age, bustling about trying to yank an extra minute or two out of already strained hours, we end up thinking rest is a luxury we can't afford. But that's a dead end. Rest is as much a gift for our renewal as grace is a gift for our redemption. The Gift of Rest isn't just for those tired of being tired. It's for those who don't know what they're missing trying to do it all."

—Dr. Cole Huffman, Senior Pastor, First Evangelical Church, Memphis, Tennessee

The Gift of Rest rocked my world! I often feel like the clown in the circus spinning plates on tall poles— three kids, high-school ministry, school PTA, and my church women's ministry. I am always busy! Crickett's study taught me that when I trust and obey God, my soul finds rest. In this busy phase of life, I'm striving to embrace the gift of rest.

—Bethany Scoggins, busy mom, Women's Ministry leader, and Young Life leader

The Gift of Rest is simple to follow, yet full of rich, biblical teaching. Crickett points readers to Scripture so they can discover for themselves why rest is important and then develop an action plan to implement it in their busy lives. An excellent resource for personal use or in a small group.

—Sue Hume, Women's Ministry Leader, Grace Church, Eden Prairie, Minnesota

ACKNOWLEDGMENTS

Special thanks to:

- The women of the Heart to Heart Bible Study at First Evangelical Church in Memphis—for encouraging me to write the Bible studies and for serving as a test group, giving valuable input.
- Sandra Glahn—for believing in me and mentoring me as a writer.
- Jim Davis and Sue Hume—for your friendship and encouragement to keep writing.
- My mom, who's with her Savior now—for always pointing me to my Savior, Jesus Christ.
- Rick Bates and CrossLink Publishing—for your encouragement and expertise throughout this process.
- Susan Nelson and Carol Newman—for your proofing and editing.
- My prayer warriors—without you, this work would not have been completed.

How to Make the Most of This Study

Each week's lesson provides five days of study. Each day contains three sections.

- **Looking to God's Word** directs you to the Scripture for that day, guiding you through observation and interpretation questions.
- **Looking Upward** challenges you to wrestle with thought-provoking questions and promotes group discussion.
- **Looking Reflectively** focuses on application and reflection. This area of the study encourages you to take head knowledge and make it heart knowledge, applying it to daily life.
- **Looking Deeper** is offered on some days as an option to look at additional passages that take you deeper into the meaning of the lesson.

To get the most out of this study, take time each day to do a lesson and reflect on the passage and main thought(s), allowing God's Spirit to speak to you and work in you through His Word to transform your life.

CONTENTS

A Personal Note

If I could be anything other than a human, I'd love to be a cat. I live with a cat, and I can tell you from firsthand experience that cats have mastered the art of rest. My cat Peyton leisurely walks over to eat from her bowl. When she's satisfied, she finds a comfortable spot where she can lie down to rest. She may play for a while, but she soon returns to a cozy spot to rest a little more.

She doesn't worry about food, shelter, or what fur she's going to wear the next day—she just rests because she's secure in my care of her. She knows I love her and I'm going to look after her. When she sits beside me purring I know she's at rest, regardless of what's going on around her. My cat has mastered rest. I, on the other hand, have not.

Is it even possible to find rest when life seems to get busier every day and the demands just keep piling up? How can we find rest when we are overwhelmed with difficult circumstances out of our control that drain us emotionally, mentally, and physically?

As I talk with people, I hear a recurring theme: "I'm worn out. I need rest." It seems we're all running on empty, in danger of burning out. Surely that's not God's plan for our lives.

Thus I began to search the Scripture to see what God says about rest.

God took time to rest after Creation. Jesus took time to rest in the midst of His busy ministry. God told His people to rest. This mandate is throughout the Bible, from Genesis to Revelation. Rest is for our good. We need it, but why aren't we able to embrace this gift of rest?

We're good at coming up with reasons why we can't rest; reasons such as:

- I'm too busy. I don't have time to rest. If I stop to rest, I can't get everything done.
- I feel guilty if I take time to rest. People will think I'm lazy. I need to be productive.
- It's not spiritual to rest.

However, the truth is God wants us to rest. Many times we bring exhaustion and burnout upon ourselves because of decisions we make. Our priorities may be wrong or we haven't learned to say no to things God never intended for us to do.

But sometimes our exhaustion and burnout aren't because of wrong priorities or a workaholic mentality. We're exhausted because of the season of life we're in.

You may be a young mom with a house full of little kids, or a caregiver for a loved one. You may be facing an unexpected crisis that you weren't planning for, or you've had to take on extra responsibilities because of circumstances out of your control. You can quickly find yourself exhausted, not only physically, but emotionally and spiritually.

As I was studying the Scriptures to find God's perspective on rest, I was experiencing a season of no rest in my own life. For several years I was the primary caregiver for my elderly mother who was living in a nursing home here in Memphis. It was undoubtedly one of the hardest seasons of life I've gone through. I was depleted emotionally and physically, and rest wasn't part of my life.

During that time, a friend emailed me her thoughts on rest during this difficult season:

> "One thing that keeps coming to my mind … is the ladies (like you) who find themselves in circumstances that totally work against rest—unable to sleep when there is time to sleep, unable to stay focused when there are times for worship, the huge depletion that happens when we are in crisis mode (not because of lifestyle/priority choices but because of absolute necessity in caring for others). It's one thing to say, "You need to rest, take time to rest, rest is vital," but quite another when body and mind are so depleted that rest doesn't happen even when there is time. I've been there, and I know the Lord got me through it— but the process was hard."

Perhaps you're in a season of no rest today, brought on by a situation that's out of your control, and you know that reordering priorities or saying no isn't going to bring rest. How do you and I find rest in these seasons of life? Is it even possible?

Yes, it is. We may not be able to experience the physical rest we desire, but we can still find rest in those times of no rest—soul rest. We find that soul rest by spending time in His Word and in His presence.

I pray that as you begin this Bible study, you would embrace the gift of rest. As you come to understand God's desire and purpose for rest, I pray that you would find joy, not guilt.

Come away to a quiet place. Be still before the One who gives rest. Slow down, listen, and enjoy life the way He intended. Embrace the gift of rest. Let's begin …

Resting in Him,

Crickett

WEEK 1

THE MODEL OF REST

"Rest" … I'm not even sure that word exists in my vocabulary. Yes, I want to rest and I need to rest, but I find it hard to actually do it. My life has been challenging over the past year—with an elderly parent and the challenges that go with that, my own health concerns, and a busy job/ministry. I long for rest. And as I talk with many around me, I hear the same longing. We need rest. Because rest seems foreign to most of us, I decided to write a study on this topic. My prayer is that God will show us through His Word how to rest in the way He intended for us to.

We begin our study of rest with the account of Creation. After six days of creating, God took a day to rest. But how often do we read the Creation story and quickly gloss over the statement that God rested? What can and should we learn from that? Even though you are probably very familiar with the Creation story, read it as if for the first time, asking God to reveal to you fresh truth from His Word.

DAY 1: GOD'S WORK, THE CREATION

LOOKING TO GOD'S WORD

1. Read all of Genesis 1. How is the earth described in Genesis 1:2?

2. As you look at the six days of creation, list what God created each day and His response to each day's work.

   Day 1:

   Day 2:

   Day 3:

   Day 4:

   Day 5:

   Day 6:

3. At the end of the sixth day, God noted that all He had created was "very good," in contrast to "good" on the previous days. What was different on this day?

4. List all the verbs used with God in this chapter. (For instance, God said, God separated.)

5. How would you describe the manner in which God created the heavens and the earth?

LOOKING UPWARD

6. If God is Creator of the world and the universe (and He is), what are the implications for us?

LOOKING REFLECTIVELY

Psalm 8:3–8

[3]*When I consider Your heavens, the work of Your fingers, The moon and the stars, which You have ordained;* [4]*What is man that You take thought of him, And the son of man that You care for him?* [5]*Yet You have made him a little lower than God, And You crown him with glory and majesty!* [6]*You make him to rule over the works of Your hands; You have put all things under his feet,* [7]*All sheep and oxen, And also the beasts of the field,* [8]*The birds of the heavens and the fish of the sea, Whatever passes through the paths of the seas.*

- Write down your thoughts as you ponder the significance of these words.

DAY 2: HUMANITY'S WORK

God created us to do more than sit around and do nothing. He gave Adam work and purpose, and He created us to work and carry out the purpose He gave us. Today we will look at the work God gave Adam in the Garden of Eden. Let God teach you through His Word today.

LOOKING TO GOD'S WORD

1. Read Genesis 1 again. How do the fifth and sixth days (1:20–31) differ from the first four days?

2. What do you observe about God's creation of us in Genesis 1:26–31?

3. What words are repeated in these verses? What might be the significance of the repetition?

4. What is God's purpose for us according to Genesis 1:26–28?

5. What additional insight do these verses give concerning Adam's work?

    Genesis 2:15

    Genesis 2:19–20

6. How do you see God's provision for humanity through creation?

LOOKING UPWARD

7. Why do you think God gave us something to do (work), instead of creating us to just sit and enjoy creation?

LOOKING REFLECTIVELY

"Virtually any job, no matter how grueling or tedious—any job that is not criminal or sinful—can be a gift from God, through God, and to God. The work of our hands, by the alchemy of our devotion, becomes the worship of our hearts." [1]

- What work has God given to you for today, for this season? How do you view it? Is it something you begrudge, or do you see it as a gift from God that leads you to worship Him?

---

[1] Mark Buchanan, *The Gift of Rest* (Nashville: Thomas Nelson, 2006), 24-25.

5

DAY 3: GOD'S REST

God created for six days and then rested. He ceased from His work of creating. This is the first time in Scripture that the concept of rest is introduced. What does God want to teach you about rest from today's lesson?

LOOKING TO GOD'S WORD

1. Read Genesis 2:1–3. List your observations from these verses. What did God do? When? Why?

2. According to Genesis 2:3, "God blessed the seventh day and sanctified it because in it He rested from all His work which God had created and made." What do you think it means that God blessed and sanctified the seventh day?

3. What words or phrases are repeated in these three verses?

4. Why do you think God rested on the seventh day? (He obviously wasn't tired as God never grows weary.)

5. What are some principles we can learn from the example of God's work and rest?

LOOKING UPWARD

6. Are you following God's example of taking a day off in seven days to rest from your work? If not, what is hindering you?

7. What would a day of rest look like for you? What do you think God would want you to include in and exclude from a day of rest?

8. What do you think God might have done on His day of rest after six days of creation?

LOOKING REFLECTIVELY

"God rested from His creative activity on the seventh day. This is not the rest that follows weariness but the rest of satisfaction and completion of a job well done. Although God did not command us to keep the Sabbath at this time, He taught the principle of one day of rest in seven." [2]

"In Genesis 2:3, the verb 'rested' is usually translated 'and sanctified it.' It means 'to make something holy; to set something apart; to distinguish it.' On the literal level, the phrase means essentially that God made this day different. But within the context of the Law, it means that the day belonged to God; it was for rest from ordinary labor, worship, and spiritual service. The day belonged to God." [3]

- What can you do or not do that would insure that your day of rest belongs to God?

---

[2] William MacDonald, *Believer's Bible Commentary: Old and New Testaments* (Nashville: Thomas Nelson, 1995), Genesis 2:1–3.

[3] *The NET Bible First Edition Notes* (Biblical Studies Press, 2006), Genesis 2:3.

DAY 4: APPLICATION

Today, we are going to focus on application for this passage in Genesis. Dr. Howard Hendricks introduced me to this eight-question method in seminary, and I have used it often in my personal study. Ask God to teach you personal lessons to apply to your own life.

LOOKING TO GOD'S WORD

Take the Genesis 1:1–2:3 passage and ask these questions:

1. Is there a sin to avoid or confess?

2. Is there a command to obey?

3. Is there a promise to claim?

4. Is there a prayer to repeat?

5. Is there an example to follow?

6. Is there a warning to consider?

7. What does it teach me about God?

8. How can I apply this to my life?

LOOKING UPWARD

9. What does taking time to rest show about the way we view God and our relationship with Him?

LOOKING REFLECTIVELY

"What are we talking about when we talk about God's rest? That He was tired mentally, tired physically? No. Simply that He ceased, He ceased creating and then was, as it were, sitting back and just being satisfied with what He had created.

He was enjoying it. He was delighting in it.... How refreshing it must have been, how delightful, how well pleased God must have been when He saw the created universe free from sin, free from decay, free from the curse, no death, no decay....

Every week of our lives we go through a cycle that is intended by God to remind us that He created the world in six days and rested. Every time a seventh day passes, we should be acknowledging God as our creator. That's a memorial to a completed creation." [4] - *John MacArthur*

- How can taking time to stop and rest deepen your relationship with God? How have you seen that to be true in your own life?

- What are some other benefits of rest?

---

[4] John MacArthur, "The Rest of Creation," Genesis 2:1–3, August 29, 1999 http://www.gty.org/Resources/Sermons/90-221 (Accessed July 24, 2013).

DAY 5: STRENGTH FOR THE WEARY

We all get tired and weary, and there are days we question if we're going to have the strength to keep on. But God wants us to turn to Him when we are weary. We are to look to Him for strength. Are you tired and weary today? Let God encourage you through this passage in Isaiah 40.

LOOKING TO GOD'S WORD

1. Today we are going to focus on Isaiah 40:21–31. Read this passage through all at once, writing down God's names.

2. What do you learn about God from this passage?

3. How does God take care of His creation?

4. How can you apply this passage to your life?

5. God does not become weary or tired (40:28), but we do. How does this passage encourage us when we're weary, and what should we do?

6. Write out Jeremiah 31:25.

LOOKING UPWARD

7. Why would focusing on God as Creator lead us to rest?

8. In what ways does God refresh you?

LOOKING REFLECTIVELY

God did not rest because of fatigue but because of His accomplishment. God is never weary. The verb translated as **rested** *(Heb.* shabat*) is related to the word for Sabbath (Heb.* shabbat*), which means "rest." Many assume that the basic meaning of the Sabbath is worship, but this is not the case. By God's blessed inactivity on this seventh day, He showed that He was satisfied with the work He had done.*[5]

Psalm 104:24–35

- Describe the relationship between the Creator and His creation. Spend some time praising Him.

---

[5] Earl D. Radmacher, Ron B. Allen, and H.W. House, *Nelson's New Illustrated Bible Commentary* (Nashville: Thomas Nelson Publishers, 1999), Gen. 2:2.

WEEK 2

THE INTRODUCTION OF REST

As we saw last week, God created for six days and took the seventh day to rest. This week we are going to look at a passage that shows God's desire for mankind to follow His example of taking a day of rest. This passage records the earliest Sabbath observance by God's people, after God brought the Israelites out from slavery in Egypt.

DAY 1: GRUMBLE, GRUMBLE, GRUMBLE

I would guess that every one of us has grumbled about something. Perhaps you are grumbling today. The sons of Israel knew how to grumble and did it often. Ask God to teach you today through the example of the sons of Israel.

LOOKING TO GOD'S WORD

1. Read Exodus 16:1–7. Where are they and how long had it been since they left Egypt (16:1)?

2. Describe the situation here. Who are the characters in this passage?

3. What do you observe about the grumbling of the sons of Israel? Why were they grumbling?

4. What does their grumbling reveal about them and their perspective?

5. What were the instructions for gathering the "bread from heaven" (16:4-5)?

LOOKING UPWARD

6. Exodus 16:2 tells us they were grumbling against Moses and Aaron. Verse 7 tells us they were grumbling against the Lord. Why is grumbling against someone actually grumbling against the Lord?

7. When are we tempted to grumble? Why do we grumble?

8. What does our grumbling reveal about us?

LOOKING REFLECTIVELY

"This means that we trust all that the love of God does; all He gives, and all He does not give; all He says, and all He does not say. To it all we say, by His loving enabling, I trust. Let us be content with our Lord's will, and tell Him so, and not disappoint Him by wishing for anything He does not give. The more we understand His love, the more we trust."[6] *—Amy Carmichael*

- How are you doing today in the area of grumbling? Are you grumbling about something? Are you discontent with your present circumstances? Confess any area in which you are grumbling against God and/or another.

- What are some practical things you can do when you find yourself grumbling that would turn you from a grumbler to a contented follower of Christ?

---

[6] Amy Carmichael, *Edges of His Ways* (Fort Washington, PA: Christian Literature Crusade, 1989), October 9.

DAY 2: GOD'S RESPONSE TO THEIR GRUMBLING

God heard the grumbling of the sons of Israel, and He did something about it—but not necessarily what they wanted. We are often like the Israelites, grumbling about our situation, but still not pleased when God handles it differently than we had envisioned.

LOOKING TO GOD'S WORD

1. Read Exodus 16:8–12. What word(s) are repeated?

2. How did God respond to their grumbling in verses 4–5 and 11–12?

3. How would the meat and bread show the sons of Israel that God is the Lord their God (16:12)?

4. What do these verses indicate about grumbling or complaining?

    Philippians 2:14-16

    James 5:9

LOOKING DEEPER (Optional)

*   Read Numbers 14, which describes the attitude of the sons of Israel later when the men returned from spying out the land. What do you observe about the Israelites here? How did God respond to them?

LOOKING UPWARD

5. How do you define grumbling?

6. What results from grumbling?

7. If we grumble long enough, like the sons of Israel, will God eventually give us what we want? Explain your answer. Can you give Scripture to support your answer?

LOOKING REFLECTIVELY

"Biblical contentment comes from within our hearts. To be internally satisfied and at rest within means that what happens to us on the outside in external circumstances doesn't destroy our restful joy inside." [7]

- Our rest within comes from Christ living in us through the Holy Spirit. Are you at rest within, or are you grumbling about your circumstances? If you're tempted to grumble, write down what it is about your circumstances that is causing you to grumble. Ask Him to teach you contentment with where He has you. Will you trust Him to do what is best for you?

---

[7] Denise George, *A Woman's Right to Rest* (Abilene, TX: Leafwood Publishers, 2012), 122.

DAY 3: INSTRUCTIONS AND DISOBEDIENCE

God provided for His people and gave them instructions on how to handle His provision. But, there were some who disobeyed. Perhaps they were curious to see what would happen, or they thought they knew better, or they didn't believe God. There were consequences to their disobedience. And there are consequences when we disobey and distrust God's Word. Again, let us learn from the mistakes of the Israelites.

LOOKING TO GOD'S WORD

1. Read Exodus 16:13–21. How did God provide for the needs of the sons of Israel?

2. Describe the manna.

3. What were God's instructions concerning the manna and how they should gather it?

4. What was the purpose of His instructions?

5. How did the sons of Israel respond to God's instructions in Exodus 16:20–21?

6. What does their response reveal about them? Why do you think they responded the way they did?

LOOKING UPWARD

7. What do you think God was trying to teach them through His instructions concerning the manna? Why didn't He just make the manna so it would not spoil for several days?

8. What helps you remember that God is your Provider? What Scriptures remind you that He provides?

LOOKING REFLECTIVELY

God gave the sons of Israel manna every day to sustain them, but it was a temporary sustenance. Later we see that Jesus came to be the Bread of life. Read John 6:31–35. What do you learn about the "bread of God"?

- Write out these verses and meditate on them.

  Deuteronomy 2:7

  Deuteronomy 8:3

- Thank Him for being the Bread of life. Are you looking to Him for sustenance or to something or someone else? If you aren't satisfied, why do you think that's true?

DAY 4: THE FIRST DAY OF REST OBSERVED

Exodus 16 makes several significant contributions to the developing doctrine of the Sabbath. First, it is the first occurrence of the term *Sabbath* in the Bible. Second, it is the first time in the Bible that Israel is commanded to observe a Sabbath practice of any kind. Here, the practice is specifically related to resting from the work of gathering manna. Third, manna was not to be gathered on the seventh day because it was a "Sabbath to the Lord" (Exodus 16:23, 26).[8]

LOOKING TO GOD'S WORD

1. Read Exodus 16:22–30. What were the instructions concerning the manna on the sixth day and why?

2. What was the situation with the manna on the seventh day, the Sabbath?

3. In Exodus 16:27, we learn that some of the people went out on the seventh day to gather, but found no manna. What does this show us about them? Why would they do that?

4. How do we respond to God in similar ways?

5. What do you learn about the Sabbath and God's view of the Sabbath from this passage?

---

[8] Bob Deffinbaugh, *The Meaning of the Sabbath*, http://www.bible.org/seriespage/meaning-sabbath-exodus-208-11 (accessed 5/10/2013).

LOOKING UPWARD

6. Write out Exodus 16:30. What did that look like for the sons of Israel? What would that look like for us today?

LOOKING REFLECTIVELY

"Sabbath is turning over to God all those things—our money, our work, our status, our reputations, our plans, our projects—that we're otherwise tempted to hold tight in our own closed fists, hold on to for dear life.... It is letting go, for one day out of seven, all those parts of our identities and abilities in which we are constantly tempted to find our security and discovering afresh that we are His children and that He is our Father and shield and defender."[9]

- Taking time to rest demonstrates that we trust God to take care of us and to accomplish what concerns us. Some of the sons of Israel had trouble taking the seventh day off from gathering manna. What does God want to teach you from today's passage?

---

[9]   Buchanan, *The Rest of God*, 98.

DAY 5: APPLICATION

LOOKING TO GOD'S WORD

Today we are going to review the passage from this week's lesson, Exodus 16:1–30. Look at the Exodus passage and answer these questions:

1. Is there a sin to avoid or confess?

2. Is there a command to obey?

3. Is there a promise to claim?

4. Is there a prayer to repeat?

5. Is there an example to follow?

6. Is there a warning to consider?

7. What does it teach me about God?

8. How can I apply this passage to my life?

LOOKING REFLECTIVELY

Psalm 78 gives us another look at the sons of Israel and their response to God. Yet, God always provided. Read through this psalm and describe the sons of Israel. How did they respond to God? Write down God's attributes that are evident in this psalm. How did He respond to the sons of Israel?

- How do we show our lack of trust in God? Thank Him that He is faithful to us in spite of our sins. Thank Him that He has covered our sins with the blood of Christ.

WEEK 3

THE COMMAND TO REST

It seems many of us look at rest as an option, something we will do if we find time for it. But that was not God's view of rest in the Old Testament (and New Testament, as we will see later). God knows how important it is. So He commanded His people to rest. If we don't, we most likely will face negative consequences—burnout, physical problems, relational problems, and loss of our passion for things that once energized us. As we look at this command to rest in the Old Testament, let us grasp how serious God is about our rest.

DAY 1: THE TEN COMMANDMENTS

God gave us the model of resting in Genesis 2. He instructed the sons of Israel in Exodus 16 to rest on the seventh day, making it a Sabbath holy to Him by refraining from gathering manna. This week, we are going to look at the command to keep the Sabbath holy and what that meant for them then and what it means for us today. We begin by looking at the Ten Commandments as a whole. Later, we will look specifically at the commandment concerning the Sabbath and rest.

LOOKING TO GOD'S WORD

1. Read Exodus 20:1–17. List the Ten Commandments.

    1.

    2.

    3.

    4.

    5.

    6.

    7.

    8.

    9.

    10.

2. Now go back and beside the commandments in Exodus 20:2–12, write the reason God gave for keeping each commandment.

3. Why do you think God only gave reasons for keeping the first five commandments?

4. What areas of life are covered in these commands?

LOOKING UPWARD

5. We are to have no other gods before us or make an idol of anything. How do you define an idol?

6. What are some examples of modern-day idols? Ask God to reveal to you any idols of varying kinds and degrees in your own life.

7. What would be some clues that would reveal you have an idol in your life?

8. If you do have idols in your life, what do you need to do to get rid of them?

9. In what ways do we take the Lord's name in vain?

10. What does it mean to honor your father and mother? How does that look as we become adults?

LOOKING REFLECTIVELY

Reflect on Hebrews 10:1–10. What does this passage say about the Law?

What does this passage say about the sacrifices of the Old Testament? The sacrifice of Jesus?

The purpose of the Law of Moses (the Ten Commandments) was to show the people their sinfulness. Only shed blood could cover sin. Today, the Word of God still reveals our sinfulness, but thankfully, our sins are covered by the shed blood of Jesus Christ once for all if we have put our trust in Him as Savior.

- Take some time to look back through the Ten Commandments and ask God to reveal to you any unconfessed sin. Confess it and thank Him that He has forgiven your sin through His shed blood on the cross.

DAY 2: REMEMBER THE SABBATH

Today we're going to focus on the commandment to remember the Sabbath day and keep it holy. This is the first commandment that doesn't begin with "You shall not." It is instruction to do something instead of refraining from doing something, although that is included in the explanation.

LOOKING TO GOD'S WORD

1. Exodus 20:8–11 focuses on the one commandment concerning the Sabbath. List your observations about this command in these verses. Ask the observation questions:

   • What

   • Who

   • When

   • Why

   • How

2. List all the verbs that detail what God did in Exodus 20:11.

3. Deuteronomy 5:1–21 restates the Ten Commandments. Write down any additional observations concerning the Sabbath from Deuteronomy 5:12–15.

29

4. What is the point of Deuteronomy 5:15? What is the connection between being delivered from Egypt and observing the Sabbath?

5. Notice in Exodus 20, God said, "**Remember** the Sabbath day." In Deuteronomy 5, He said, "**Observe** the Sabbath day." Is there a difference between *remember* and *observe* and if so, what do you think it might be?

6. In Deuteronomy 5:12–15, the Lord associated the Sabbath with Israel's deliverance from Egypt. How is this a foretaste of the rest they would enjoy in their promised inheritance according to these verses?

    •   Deuteronomy 3:18–20

    •   Deuteronomy 12:10

    •   Deuteronomy 25:19

LOOKING UPWARD

7. What does it mean that God made the Sabbath day holy? What does *holy* mean?

8. God told them to labor and do **all** their work in six days so they could rest on the seventh day (Deut. 5:13–14). How would you answer the person who says, "I have to work seven days straight because I have too much work to do. There is no way I can get it **all** done in six days"?

LOOKING REFLECTIVELY

"Does the Sabbath have to be exactly twenty-four hours? Must it be celebrated on Sunday or on Saturday? Could it begin on Saturday a half hour before dusk and end Sunday at near the same time? These questions too often take us far from the true heart of what it means to celebrate the Sabbath. The Sabbath is simply not a day to 'perform' religious activities and then to claim the rest of the day for thoughtless routine or mere entertainment or diversions. It doesn't matter what day you enter the Sabbath. Many who minister in our churches as pastors may celebrate the Sabbath on Monday or Friday... The issue is not when or how long, but if a day is at all chosen for delight." —Dan Allender [10]

- Do you take time each week to delight in the Lord, His creation, and His work around you? Take some time today to delight in Him.

---

[10] Dan Allender, *Sabbath: The Ancient Practices* (Nashville: Thomas Nelson, 2009), 8–9.

DAY 3: THE IMPORTANCE OF THE SABBATH

Today we are going to look at other Old Testament passages that talk about what should and shouldn't be done on the Sabbath. God made it clear that keeping the Sabbath was important to Him. This is the first time He refers to it as a "perpetual covenant" with Israel.

LOOKING TO GOD'S WORD

1. According to Exodus 23:10–12, what was the purpose of taking a break on the seventh year and seventh day?

2. What was significant about observing the Sabbath according to Exodus 31:12–17?

3. What were the reasons God gave for observing the Sabbath?

4. Why is God's name in Exodus 31:13, "The Lord who sanctifies you," *Yahweh M'Kaddesh*, appropriate in this setting?

5. What would result if someone didn't observe the Sabbath?

6. What other observations do you make about rest and the Sabbath from the Exodus 31 passage?

LOOKING UPWARD

7. My senior pastor, Cole Huffman, taught on the discipline of rest several years ago. He commented, "In my interpretation

of Scripture, the New Testament church is not bound to the Mosaic practice of Sabbath-keeping as a rule. But we do still need the principle; we still need a Sabbath day kind of rest."[11] What would that look like to you?

LOOKING REFLECTIVELY

"The idea of taking Sabbath or finding time to rest is an invitation to rest and renew yourself. The Sabbath asks us to take a break from a busy schedule and never-ending 'to-do' list and take one day to rest our souls, reorder our worlds, and realign ourselves with God." [12]

- Are you taking some extended, unhurried time each week to rest and renew yourself from your busy schedule?

- Set aside some special time with the Lord this week to sit in His presence, meditate on his Word, asking Him to renew you, refresh you, and reorder things in your life.

- Lord, what would you have me do that I'm not doing?

- Lord, what do I need to stop doing that you never intended for me to do?

---

[11] Cole Huffman, Sermon titled *The Role of Classic Spiritual Disciplines in Loving God: Rest, A Discipline of Abstinence*; Given August 31, 2008 to First Evangelical Church in Memphis, TN.

[12] Margaret Feinberg, *Resting in Him: I need to slow down but I can't!* (Nashville: Thomas Nelson, 2008), 23.

DAY 4: ADDITIONAL PASSAGES CONCERNING THE SABBATH

Today we will look at a few more Old Testament passages that refer to the Sabbath. Repetition indicates emphasis. God obviously wanted to emphasize the importance of keeping the Sabbath and taking a day of rest.

LOOKING TO GOD'S WORD

1. What does God say about rest in Exodus 34:21?

2. He commands them to rest even during plowing time and harvest. How would that relate to us today in the twenty-first century? What principle can we draw from that?

3. List your observations concerning Sabbath rest from Exodus 35:2–3.

4. Why do you think the specific task of kindling a fire was singled out in Exodus 35:3?

5. What were the commands in Leviticus 26:2?

LOOKING UPWARD

6. How would you define "Sabbath rest" according to the Old Testament? What would that day look like according to God's instructions?

7. Why do you think Sabbath rest was so important to God?

LOOKING REFLECTIVELY

"Nine of the Ten Commandments are repeated in the New Testament epistles for the church to obey; the exception is the fourth commandment (Deuteronomy 5:12–15) about the Sabbath Day. Why? The Sabbath Day was a special sign between Israel and the Lord ... and wasn't given to any other nation...." [13]

As my pastor Cole Huffman said, even though we as believers today are not bound to the Mosaic practice of Sabbath-keeping as a rule, we still need the principle of taking a Sabbath day rest. Some people take it literally, saying that we should do absolutely nothing on that day. But is that moving toward legalism?

I like what Cole said about this: "For us, the accent in our resting should be not on doing nothing when you rest, though you are welcome to do nothing. But our accent in resting should be on doing what you don't have to do—that is setting aside a portion of a day, or better, an entire day that is protected from the tyranny of the urgent. A day that will not be rushed." [14]

- What activity would replenish you?

- What is your perspective of Sabbath rest? Are you satisfied with how your understanding of Sabbath rest matches your actions? Are there some changes you'd like to make?

---

[13] Warren Wiersbe, *The Bible Exposition Commentary: Pentateuch* (Colorado Springs: Victor Books, 2001), 385.

[14] Cole Huffman, *Rest, A Discipline of Abstinence*; Sermon given August 31, 2008 to First Evangelical Church.

DAY 5: A SONG FOR THE SABBATH

Psalm 92 is subtitled, "A Psalm, a Song for the Sabbath Day." It is suggestive of the kinds of worship activities appropriate on the Sabbath day.

LOOKING TO GOD'S WORD

1. Read Psalm 92 and write down the kinds of worship activities pointed out in this psalm.

2. What does the psalmist say about God and who He is? Which attributes of God does he focus on?

3. What should be our response as we focus on who God is?

LOOKING UPWARD

4. Why would this be an appropriate song for the Sabbath day?

5. What principles can we glean from this for today?

6. How would focusing on God and who He is help us rest?

LOOKING REFLECTIVELY

Mark Buchanan, in *The Rest of God*, recommends practicing the sovereignty of God. His instructions are: "Today when you pray, start with God. Survey what he has made. Recite what he has done. Proclaim who he is."[15]

- Spend some time praising God, contemplating His greatness and His sovereignty over everything in and around your life.

---

[15] Buchanan, *The Rest of God*, 75.

WEEK 4

THE PROVISION OF REST

We think of rest in different ways. We rest when we're tired. We rest in the Lord when we're anxious. We rest on God's promises. We rest in God's protection from spiritual warfare and enemies of the world. This week, we're going to look at some of the ways God provides rest for us.

DAY 1: RESTING IN GOD'S PRESENCE

We are going to spend several days focusing on this area. As we spend time alone in His presence, we can draw strength for any situation we may be facing. He has a calming effect on us as we pour out our hearts to Him.

LOOKING TO GOD'S WORD

Exodus 33:12–16

1. What two things did God promise Moses and the sons of Israel in Exodus 33:14?

2. Why was God's presence so important to Moses?

Psalm 16:7–11

3. What does David say he has done and will do?

4. What has God done and will do?

5. What do you think David meant when he said, "I have set the Lord continually before me" in Psalm 16:8?

6. Confidence in God leads to rest. Why is David able to have such confidence in God?

LOOKING UPWARD

7. In Psalm 16:11, David says, "In Your presence is fullness of joy." As a Christian, we are always in God's presence because His Spirit indwells us. If that is true, then why is that joy not always evident?

LOOKING REFLECTIVELY

"In David's case, his battles were won in his private times of worship with the Lord. David had many responsibilities, and there were many demands upon his time; but his number one priority was seeking God's face.... Wherever he was, he took time to come into God's presence, meditate on God's gracious kindness, and contemplate the person of God." [16] — Warren Wiersbe

- Take some time today to follow David's example. Seek God's face and enjoy sitting in His presence. Be quiet and still. "Meditate on God's gracious kindness and contemplate the person of God."

---

[16] Warren Wiersbe, *Meet Yourself in the Psalms* (Wheaton: Victor, 1986), 113–114.

DAY 2: GOD'S PRESENCE—ALWAYS THERE

I drove home one afternoon in tears from the nursing home where my mom lives, asking God, "Are You even aware of what's going on in my life? It seems like You aren't even involved in this." The next morning, God took me to Psalm 139 and reminded me of His intimate involvement in my life, even when it feels like He's distant or too busy with someone else's problems. I needed Psalm 139 to bring things back into perspective. Maybe you're feeling God is uninvolved and distant. Let this psalm refresh you as it did me. He reminded me that He is always with me and knows everything going on in my life, even when it seems He is silent. Thank You, Father.

LOOKING TO GOD'S WORD
Psalm 139:1-12

1. How is God's presence portrayed in these verses?

2. Take each phrase and write what it means to you.

   - You have searched me and known me (139:1)

   - You know when I sit down and when I rise up (139:2)

   - You understand my thought from afar (139:2)

   - You scrutinize my path and my lying down (139:3)

   - You are intimately acquainted with all my ways (139:3)

- Even before there is a word on my tongue. You know it all (139:4)

- You have enclosed me behind and before, and laid Your hand upon me (139:5)

3. How do these verses give you rest in the midst of your own difficult circumstances?

LOOKING UPWARD

4. Suppose someone tells you she doesn't feel God's presence anymore and feels all alone in a situation; she feels God is distant and uninvolved and she isn't able to find rest in Him. How would you respond?

LOOKING REFLECTIVELY

"Let us resolve at once that it will be the one characteristic of our life and worship, a continual, humble, truthful waiting on God. We may rest assured that He who made us for Himself, that He might give Himself to us and in us, that He will never disappoint us. In waiting on Him, we will find rest and joy and strength, and the supply of every need." [17]

Are you in the middle of a hard situation today? Turn to Him, go to His Word, wait on Him, and find rest in Him, knowing that He is intimately acquainted with all that is going on in your life.

Spend some time praying or writing out a prayer, expressing the cry of your heart. But be still and wait on God, resting in His presence. Read a verse or passage out loud and meditate on it. God's Word is powerful.

---

[17] Andrew Murray, *Waiting on God* (New Kensington, PA: Whitaker House, 1983), 21.

DAY 3: STRENGTH AND COURAGE IN GOD'S PRESENCE

We've been looking at finding rest in God's presence. Today we are going to look at God's promise to Moses, the Israelites, and Joshua as they prepared to enter the land of Canaan. There are times in life when we face obstacles that seem insurmountable, and it's hard to rest when we don't know what's ahead of us. But God invites us to rest in His strength and His presence.

LOOKING TO GOD'S WORD

Deuteronomy 31:1–8

1. Moses is near the end of his life and gives his last counsel to the people and to Joshua. What does he instruct them to do?

2. What does he emphasize about God and His character?

3. How would this encourage you as you face an overwhelming situation?

Joshua 1:1–15

4. In Joshua 1, Joshua takes over the leadership of the sons of Israel and begins the process of taking the land God promised them. What promises does God give to Joshua?

5. What does God instruct Joshua to do?

6. What kind of rest does God promise them?

LOOKING UPWARD

7. Which attributes of God most encourage and strengthen you when you are facing an overwhelming situation and struggle to rest in the midst of it?

8. How does knowing that God will never leave you nor forsake you give you rest?

LOOKING REFLECTIVELY

- Are you finding rest in God's presence? If not, what is hindering you?

- Take some time to read back over one of the passages from today's lesson. Meditate on it. Thank God that He never leaves you and He will strengthen you to do what He has called you to do.

DAY 4: RESTING IN THE SHEPHERD'S CARE

Psalm 23 is a well-loved psalm that many have memorized. This psalm has a calming, soothing effect on those who read and hear these words. Today we are going to look at the first three verses that focus on rest given by the Shepherd. Will you embrace that rest or ignore it?

LOOKING TO GOD'S WORD

Psalm 23:1–3

1. What are the four things God does to give us rest in these verses?

2. "He makes me lie down in green pastures." What does that mean to you? How does God do that?

3. "He leads me beside quiet waters." What does that mean to you? How would this provide rest for you?

4. In what ways does God restore your soul? Can you think of Scriptures that talk about this?

5. How does God's guidance give you rest?

LOOKING UPWARD

6. Which of these four things are you drawing rest from today?

7. Are you resisting His provision in any of these areas? If so, how?

LOOKING REFLECTIVELY

Reflect on Jesus' words in John 10:11–15. How does knowing that Jesus is your Shepherd give you rest?

"We live a most uncertain life. Any hour can bring disaster, danger, and distress from unknown quarters… We live either in a sense of anxiety, fear, and foreboding, or in a sense of quiet rest… Then in the midst of our misfortunes there suddenly comes the awareness that He, the Christ, the Good Shepherd, is there. It makes all the difference. His presence in the picture throws a different light on the whole scene." [18] — Phillip Keller

• Write a psalm of praise to your Shepherd.

---

[18] Phillip Keller, *A Shepherd Looks at Psalm 23* (Grand Rapids: Zondervan, 1970), 38.

DAY 5: REST THROUGH GOD'S PEOPLE

God wants us to spend time alone with Him and look to Him for strength and guidance. He wants us to be dependent on Him, not others. Yet, He also provides the body of Christ for us. We are part of a community of believers, and there is value in spending time with other believers. God uses others to refresh us and give us rest in times of stress and turmoil. Today we are going to look at some examples of this from the New Testament. Ask God to speak to your heart today from His Word.

LOOKING TO GOD'S WORD

2 Corinthians 7:5–7

1. Why did Paul not have rest according to verse 5?

2. How did God encourage and comfort him?

3. How do other believers contribute to rest in our lives according to the following passages?

    Romans 15:30–33

    Philemon 7, 17–20

    Hebrews 10:24–25

LOOKING UPWARD

4. What is the balance between looking to God for rest and looking to people? When do you know which is appropriate at a given time?

LOOKING REFLECTIVELY

- Would people describe you as someone who is refreshing to be around? If so, why? If not, why not? What needs to change in order for you to be refreshing to others?

- Ask God to develop you into the kind of person who would be refreshing to others and not draining.

I am so thankful for those people whom God has used in my life to refresh me in the midst of difficult times. Sometimes, it's someone who is in the same situation and they totally understand what I'm feeling. Or it's someone who has walked down this path before me, and they've gone through what I'm going through now. And there are those whom God has used to refresh me and are not even aware of how God has used them. But they said the very words I needed to hear for that moment. God uses others to refresh us and encourage us in those dark times. Send a note this week to someone whom God has used in your life to refresh you. Give thanks to God for them.

WEEK 5

THE LEGALISTIC VIEW OF REST

This week we are going to look at several Gospel passages that focus on Sabbath controversies. The Jews and Pharisees were accusing Jesus and His disciples of breaking the Sabbath. Jesus had a different perspective. But first we will look at a passage in Isaiah that describes how the Old Testament Jews were to honor the Sabbath.

DAY 1: HONOR THE SABBATH

Keeping the Sabbath was a measure of one's faithfulness to the Mosaic Covenant and the fourth commandment. By following the rules for the Sabbath, a person acknowledged the importance of worshipping God and showed that he depended on God to provide for his needs as he took time away from work. By choosing to put God first, he showed his trust in God's provision for his needs.

LOOKING TO GOD'S WORD

In Isaiah 58, God told Isaiah to announce the sins of the nation. The people went to the temple, obeyed God's laws, fasted, and appeared eager to seek the Lord, but their worship was only an outward show. Their hearts were far from God.[19] Today we are going to focus on just two verses from this chapter that talk about the Sabbath, but there is a lot packed into these two verses.

1. Read Isaiah 58:13–14. What does Isaiah say they should do on the Sabbath (58:13)?

2. What does it mean "to turn your foot from doing your own pleasure on My holy day"? What would that require?

3. What does it mean to call the Sabbath a delight?

4. What do you think He means by desisting from "speaking your own word" on the Sabbath?

5. What are the results of obedience to keeping the Sabbath (58:14)?

6. What does it mean to you personally to take delight in the Lord? How do you do that?

---

[19] Warren Wiersbe, Be *Comforted* (Wheaton: Victor Books, 1996), 150–151.

7. Why would taking delight in the Lord be a natural result of keeping the Sabbath?

LOOKING DEEPER (Optional)

You may want to read all of Isaiah 58. In this chapter, Isaiah talks about fasting and keeping the Sabbath and the proper attitude for both. Write down your observations from this chapter.

LOOKING UPWARD

"Ritual and ceremony had a significant place in Israel's worship of the Lord. But faith is not summed up in ritual. Too often a Christian's lifestyle can become simply following a pattern of 'religious' duties." [20]

8. How is this true in our society today—following a pattern of "religious" duties instead of truly worshipping the Lord? How is this true in your life?

LOOKING REFLECTIVELY

"It is important to keep the Sabbath for God's sake, and not just use it as an extra day off. It is a day to delight in the Lord."[21]

*   How would taking a day to delight in the Lord look for you?

---

[20] L. Richards and L.O. Richards, *The Teacher's Commentary* (Wheaton: Victor Books, 1987), 398.

[21] Andrew Knowles, *The Bible Guide* (Minneapolis: Augsburg, 2001), 292.

DAY 2: LORD OF THE SABBATH

Yesterday we looked at an Old Testament passage that described how one should honor the Sabbath. Unfortunately, the Jews in Jesus' day continued to focus on rituals and rules instead of delighting in God and what He was doing. The rest of this week we will look at two different perspectives of the Sabbath—the perspective of the Pharisees and the Jews, and the perspective of Jesus.

LOOKING TO GOD'S WORD

Matthew 12:1-7

1. What did the disciples do that upset the Pharisees?

2. Why did it upset them?

3. How did Jesus respond to the Pharisees?

4. Look back at the story of David eating the consecrated bread in 1 Samuel 21:1–6. Why would this be an appropriate response to the Pharisees' accusation that the disciples were doing something unlawful on the Sabbath?

5. There is a parallel account of this story in Mark 2:23–28. In Mark 2:27, what do you think Jesus meant when He said, "The Sabbath was made for us, and not us for the Sabbath"?

6. In what ways does Jesus, as Lord of the Sabbath, seem to be redefining the meaning of the day?

54

7. How does this relate to the situation with the Pharisees complaining about the disciples picking the heads of grain on the Sabbath?

LOOKING UPWARD

8. Do you think the disciples were really doing something that wasn't lawful on the Sabbath? Explain your answer.

9. What does it mean for us practically that Jesus is "Lord of the Sabbath" (Mark 2:27; Matthew 12:8)?

LOOKING REFLECTIVELY

The Pharisees failed to understand compassion for people's basic needs (in this case, hunger), but they were committed to their own sacrifices.

- Write out Hosea 6:6. What was the point God was making and how does it apply to the situation in Matthew 12?

- Have you become legalistic about Sundays (the day of the Lord) in any way? Do you have questions about what you should or shouldn't do on Sunday?

DAY 3: HEALING ON THE SABBATH

Today we continue our look at the Sabbath and what Jesus did on the Sabbath. The Jews were legalistic in what they thought the Sabbath should look like and what should and shouldn't be done on the Sabbath. But Jesus demonstrated a different perspective of the Sabbath.

We, like the Jews in that time, can become legalistic about Sundays. What can we learn from Jesus about this? Today, we pick up the story from where we left off yesterday.

LOOKING TO GOD'S WORD

Matthew 12:9–14

1. Where was Jesus on the Sabbath in this passage?

2. When the Pharisees asked Jesus if it was lawful to heal on the Sabbath, how did Jesus' response answer their question?

3. Read the parallel passage in Mark 3:1–6. What additional details does this passage give? How do the two passages differ?

4. What emotions did Jesus feel in Mark 3:5? Why do you think He felt this way?

5. How were the Pharisees viewing the Sabbath?

LOOKING UPWARD

6. Legalism can be obvious or subtle. What are some ways you see legalism concerning Sundays? Concerning all areas of life?

7. Jesus said in Matthew 12:12, "It is lawful to do good on the Sabbath." What do you think doing good on the Sabbath might look like in our lives?

LOOKING REFLECTIVELY

Jesus affirmed how valuable people are in this passage. What are some other verses that reaffirm how valuable you are to God? You might start with Matthew 6:25–34.

- Thank Him for His love for you and that He values you. He knows we're broken and imperfect, but He loves us and longs to make us whole.

DAY 4: A DAY TO CELEBRATE FREEDOM

Today we look at another situation concerning Jesus and the Sabbath. We meet a lady who had been in bondage for eighteen years. Jesus could have walked right by her, but He didn't. He stopped, and He freed her. And yes, He did it on the Sabbath. Let's see how the synagogue official responded to Jesus.

LOOKING TO GOD'S WORD
Luke 13:10-17

1. What is the setting for this story? When? What was Jesus doing (13:10)?

2. Describe the woman at the synagogue. What do you learn about her from this passage?

3. How did Jesus respond to her? Look for the four verbs that describe His response to her in 13:12–13.

4. After Jesus healed the woman bent over double, what was the synagogue official's response (13:14) and why?

5. What was Jesus trying to get across by His response in verses 15–16?

6. Why do you think Jesus' opponents were humiliated by His response?

LOOKING UPWARD

7. Satan had held this woman in bondage for eighteen long years. What are some ways Satan holds people in bondage today?

LOOKING REFLECTIVELY

In the Old Testament, the sons of Israel were to remember their freedom and liberation from Egypt as they observed the Sabbath. In the Luke passage, Jesus implied it is fitting that this woman be released from bondage to Satan on the Sabbath.

"Sabbath celebrates the God who frees the heart from slavery. God has not only redeemed us from Egypt, but he has turned our hearts toward eternity."[22]

*   Take some time to celebrate your freedom in Christ. Thank Him for dying on the cross for your sins and freeing you from the penalty for sin.

*   Even though Jesus has paid the debt for our sins, we still struggle with sin and bondage while we are on this earth in the flesh. Is there something you need to be set free from? Ask God to reveal to you anything that is holding you in bondage. Ask God to help you break free. What are some things you need to do and things you need to avoid in order to break free?

---

[22] Allender, *Sabbath: The Ancient Practices*, 184.

DAY 5: GOD'S WORK

Today, we look at another situation in which Jesus healed someone on the Sabbath and the Jews accused Him of breaking the Sabbath rules. Jesus explained that He and God the Father never stop working.

LOOKING TO GOD'S WORD

John 5:1–18

1. What was the situation in verses 1–9? Go through the observation questions:

   What:

   Why:

   Who:

   How:

   Where:

   When: (5:9)

2. How did the Jews respond to what happened (5:10)?

3. How did the perspectives of the Jews and Jesus differ concerning the Sabbath?

4. How did their perspectives differ concerning the man who was sick and then healed?

5. What is significant about Jesus' answer in 5:17?

6. How are Jesus and the Father working (5:17)? (See also John 17:4.)

LOOKING UPWARD

7. Why do you think Jesus worked (healed) on the Sabbath?

8. Jesus was attentive to God the Father and the work God gave Him to do. What helps increase our attentiveness to God and the work He has given us to do?

LOOKING REFLECTIVELY

"If God stopped every kind of work on the Sabbath, nature would fall into chaos and sin would overrun the world. Genesis 2:2 says that God rested on the seventh day; He rested from the work of creation but began the work of sustaining the creation." [23]

- Take some time to list the many ways you see God at work today, this week, this month. Thank Him for what He is doing and how He is working.

---

[23] Bruce Barton, Philip Comfort, et al, *Life Application New Testament Commentary* (Wheaton: Tyndale, 2001), 394.

WEEK 6

THE BALANCE OF REST

As we saw in Genesis 1 and 2, God gave us the model of work and rest. God's work was Creation. He worked six days to create the heavens and earth and all that inhabits them. On the seventh day, He rested; not because He was tired, but to enjoy His creation and to set an example for us. This week we are going to focus on the need to balance work and rest and what Scripture has to say about it.

DAY 1: IDLENESS

Some think that rest is doing absolutely nothing. And there are times when we need to refrain from doing anything. However, resting is not necessarily the same thing as being idle. Idleness can get us into trouble. Paul talked to the Thessalonians about the balance between working and being idle. Today we will look at Paul's words to the Thessalonians.

LOOKING TO GOD'S WORD

1. What does Paul say about this issue from these verses? List your observations. (Are there commands to be followed? Are there warnings to heed? What is going on with the Thessalonians?)

    1 Thessalonians 4:9–12

    2 Thessalonians 3:6–13

2. What do these proverbs say about work, idleness, and/or rest? What results from idleness?

Proverbs 10:4–5

⁴ Poor is he who works with a negligent hand, But the hand of the diligent makes rich. ⁵ He who gathers in summer is a son who acts wisely, *But* he who sleeps in harvest is a son who acts shamefully.

Proverbs 14:23

²³ In all labor there is profit, But mere talk *leads* only to poverty.

Proverbs 20:13

¹³ Do not love sleep, or you will become poor; Open your eyes, *and* you will be satisfied with food.

Proverbs 24:30–34

³⁰ I passed by the field of the sluggard And by the vineyard of the us lacking sense, ³¹ And behold, it was completely overgrown

with thistles; Its surface was covered with nettles, And its stone wall was broken down. [32] When I saw, I reflected upon it; I looked, *and* received instruction. [33] "A little sleep, a little slumber, A little folding of the hands to rest," [34] Then your poverty will come *as a* robber And your want like an armed man.

LOOKING UPWARD

3. What draws us to idleness? Why would we want to be idle?

4. Is idleness the same as rest? Why or why not?

LOOKING REFLECTIVELY

"Evaluate your use of time now and spend it in a way that you would like to hear at the Judgment. And if you cannot answer your conscience regarding how you use your time in the growth of Christlikeness now, how will you be able to answer God then? Jonathan Edwards suggested living each day as if at the end of that day you had to give an account to God of how you used your time." [24]

*   Do you think God is pleased with how you use your time? If not, what needs to change? How will you go about implementing those changes?

---

[24]   Donald Whitney, *Spiritual Disciplines for the Christian Life* (Colorado Springs: NavPress, 1991), 130.

DAY 2: OVERWORKING

We live in a society today that pushes us to work, work, and work more. Forty-hour work weeks are beginning to be the exception now, rather than the rule. Many employers expect their employees to work 50–60 hours a week. However, I personally think we're moving into dangerous ground with this type of work ethic. Our bodies are not designed to work such long hours. Our families suffer. Friendships are neglected. Our health declines. I can't imagine God pushing Adam to work overtime in the Garden of Eden.

Today we are going to look at this area of working too much. Ask God to show you if you need to make any changes in this area or encourage someone you care about to make changes.

LOOKING TO GOD'S WORD

1. Read Exodus 18:13–24. What did Moses' father-in-law Jethro exhort him about?

2. Why was Moses' method and plan not good (18:17)? Why was Jethro concerned?

3. What was Jethro's suggestion? In what ways would this be better than what Moses was doing?

4. Solomon wrote in Psalm 127:2, "It is vain for you to rise up early, to retire late, to eat the bread of painful labors; for He gives to His beloved even in his sleep." Why would it be vain to rise up early, retire late, and to labor painfully?

5. What principles about work and rest can we learn from the story of Mary and Martha in Luke 10:38–42?

LOOKING UPWARD

6. What drives us to overwork (in job, at home, in ministry, etc.)?

7. What can we practically do to alleviate overworking?

8. What are the results of overworking?

LOOKING REFLECTIVELY

"It is not God who loads us until we bend or crack with an ulcer, nervous breakdown, heart attack, or stroke. These come from our inner compulsions coupled with the pressure of circumstances." [25]

- Are you guilty of overworking? If so, why and what can you do to stop? What do you need to change?

---

[25] Charles E. Hummel, *Tyranny of the Urgent* (Madison, WI: InterVarsity Christian Fellowship, 1967), 11.

DAY 3: GLORIFYING GOD THROUGH WORK AND REST

I am not a morning person. It doesn't matter what time I go to bed at night, I hate to hear the alarm in the morning. I have to drag myself out of bed. But once I get up and start moving, I get into my routine and I'm fine. I enjoy going to work, although there are days, I admit, I'd love to stay in my PJ's and rest. But work is good for us. Rest is good for us. And we can glorify God through both. But do we?

LOOKING TO GOD'S WORD

1. Write out the following verses. How do they encourage a balance between work and rest? List any principles you can glean from these verses concerning work.

    1 Corinthians 10:31

    Colossians 3:17

    Colossians 3:23-24

2. Paul was giving instructions to slaves in Ephesians 6:5–8. Describe how they were to serve their masters.

3. What principles about work can we apply to our own lives from this passage?

LOOKING UPWARD

4. How does your work (whatever you do) bring glory to God?

5. How would you recognize if something you're doing in your work is not glorifying God?

6. How does your rest bring glory to God?

LOOKING REFLECTIVELY

"Beware of any work for God that causes or allows you to avoid concentrating on Him. A great number of Christian workers worship their work. The only concern of Christian workers should be their concentration of God." [26]—Oswald Chambers

- Do you worship your work, whether it be a paid job, a volunteer position, or in the home?

- Write a prayer of commitment to the Lord concerning "whatever you do." Do it as unto the Lord. (John 8:28–29 is a good example at which to look.)

---

[26] Oswald Chambers, *My Utmost for His Highest, An Updated Edition in Today's Language* (Grand Rapids: Discovery House, 2010), April 23.

DAY 4: STRENGTH IN REST

When we rest, we show that we are placing our trust in God, not needing to push forward in our own efforts and strength. Instead, we turn to Him to strengthen us. However, the people of Judah had trouble with this. As we look at their response to God, let us learn from their mistakes.

LOOKING TO GOD'S WORD

In Isaiah 30, the people of Judah turned to Egypt for help against Assyria instead of trusting in God. Rather than trusting in God, they sought escape on swift horses. God was not pleased with them, but He longed to be gracious to them.

Isaiah 30:15–18

1. According to Isaiah 30:15, what should we be looking to for strength and deliverance?

2. What does God mean by, "In repentance and rest you shall be saved"?

3. What does He mean by "In quietness and trust is your strength"?

4. They were not willing to put their trust in God and rest in His strength. What was God's response to them in Isaiah 30:18?

LOOKING UPWARD

5. Why is it hard for us to rest and trust instead of working in our own efforts to see desired results in a situation?

LOOKING REFLECTIVELY

"Rest also does something powerful within our souls. When we stop, we are in a better position to allow God to move in our lives. Rest is a physical reminder that we are not in control of everything and, at the end of the day we are not the ones who have to hold it all together. That is God's job. Rest reminds us of our place, not just in life, but in Him." [27]

*   Is there something today you are feeling you need to control? Can you let it go and entrust it into God's hands? He is in control of everything that comes into our lives. We can only find true rest when we come to believe that in our hearts, not just our heads.

---

[27]   Margaret Feinberg, *Resting in Him*, 8.

DAY 5: SOLOMON'S PERSPECTIVE OF WORK AND REST

Solomon addresses work and rest throughout the Book of Ecclesiastes. Today we are going to look at some of these passages.

LOOKING TO GOD'S WORD

1. As you read Ecclesiastes 2:22–25, write down your observations about what Solomon says about work and rest.

2. Read Ecclesiastes 4:4–6. What do you think Solomon means in verse 4 when he says that every labor and skill done is the result of rivalry between a man and his neighbor? How can that lead to overworking?

3. What three scenarios does he give concerning work and rest from these verses in Ecclesiastes 4?

     Verse 5

     Verse 6a

     Verse 6b

4. Why is the "one hand full of rest better than two fists full of labor and striving after wind"(4: 6)? What does the "one hand" imply?

5. Solomon also addresses work in Ecclesiastes 5:18–20. What are your observations about work from this passage?

LOOKING UPWARD

6. How can our work be a positive thing?

7. When can our work become a negative thing?

LOOKING REFLECTIVELY

"God intends our work to be a natural expression of who we are, consistent with our inherent interests and abilities. When it isn't, we feel out of place, insignificant, and either bored or defeated. When it is, we feel like we have something important to contribute, and we're challenged without being overwhelmed." [28]

- What is something you can apply to your own life from today's lesson?

- Are you working within the areas of your strengths, gifts, and passions? If not, take steps to move in that direction. You will be energized instead of drained. If you're not sure where your strengths, gifts, and passions lie, ask God to show you clearly. What do you enjoy doing? What energizes you?

---

[28] Bill Hybels, *Honest to God? Becoming an Authentic Christian* (Grand Rapids: Zondervan, 1990), 138.

- You may find yourself in a role not allowing you to fully use your gifts and passions for a season. If so, ask God to give you contentment with where He has you in this season of life.

WEEK 7

THE DISCIPLINES OF REST

Rest does not come naturally for some of us. We have to discipline ourselves to stop and take time to rest. Just as God gave the model of resting in Genesis 2, so Jesus gave us the model of resting in the New Testament. He spent time alone with God, away from the crowds and things that needed to be done. We would do well to follow in the Savior's footsteps and allow ourselves to rest. This week we're going to look at several spiritual disciplines that can benefit our times of rest and draw us closer to the Savior.

Jan Winebrenner talks about the value of spiritual disciplines in giving us rest. She says, "The spiritual disciplines are not a rigid set of rules imposing stringent behavior practices on us. Nor do they require more tasks and activities added to already overburdened lives. The great beauty offered by the spiritual disciplines is this: they teach us how to rely on the loving sufficiency of God; they show us how to recognize His presence and revel in His sovereignty; they lead us into ever-deepening levels of intimacy with the God who calls us His 'beloved'; they teach us to allow God to work for us, in every situation. In short, they offer us rest." [29]

This week, let's take time to exercise these spiritual disciplines and find rest.

DAY 1: THE DISCIPLINE OF SOLITUDE

Today, we are going to look at the example of Jesus and how He practiced the discipline of solitude.

LOOKING TO GOD'S WORD

1. As you read the following passages, mark anything applying to solitude and rest.

   ### Matthew 14:13

   [13]Now when Jesus heard about John, He withdrew from there in a boat to a secluded place by Himself; and when the people heard of this, they followed Him on foot from the cities.

   ### Matthew 14:22–23

   [22]Immediately He made the disciples get into the boat and go ahead of Him to the other side, while He sent the crowds away.
   [23]After He had sent the crowds away, He went up on the mountain by Himself to pray; and when it was evening, He was there alone.

   ---

   [29] Jan Winebrenner, *Intimate Faith: A Woman's Guide to the Spiritual Disciplines* (New York: Warner Books, 2003), 6.

Mark 1:35

³⁵In the early morning, while it was still dark, Jesus got up, left the house, and went away to a secluded place, and was praying there.

Luke 4:42

⁴²When day came, Jesus left and went to a secluded place; and the crowds were searching for Him, and came to Him and tried to keep Him from going away from them.

Luke 5:15-16

¹⁵ But the news about Him was spreading even farther, and large crowds were gathering to hear Him and to be healed of their sicknesses. ¹⁶ But Jesus Himself would often slip away to the wilderness and pray.

Luke 6:12–13

¹²It was at this time that He went off to the mountain to pray, and He spent the whole night in prayer to God. ¹³And when day came, He called His disciples to Him and chose twelve of them, whom He also named as apostles:

2. What were some of the reasons Jesus spent time by Himself?

3. When were the various times He would slip away?

4. Where did He go?

LOOKING UPWARD

5. What important lessons for your own life do you gain from the example of Jesus' practice of solitude?

6. How would the discipline of solitude benefit you?

7. What hinders you from this discipline? What do you need to eliminate or rearrange in order to spend time daily in solitude?

8. You may be a young mom who laughs at the thought of getting any solitude. What are some creative ways you can carve out some time for solitude?

9. Some people don't like solitude. What would be some reasons why they avoid being alone?

LOOKING REFLECTIVELY

"At its heart, solitude is primarily about NOT doing something. Just as fasting means to refrain from eating, so solitude means to refrain from society. When we go into solitude, we withdraw from conversation, from the presence of others, from noise, from the constant barrage of stimulation." [30] —John Ortberg

"Yet solitude, as a spiritual discipline, calls us to keep company with God. It beckons us to carve out time in our hectic schedules to be alone with God in a quiet place. It invites us to soak in His presence and be revived and renewed." [31] —Jan Winebrenner

---

[30] John Ortberg, *The Life You've Always Wanted* (Grand Rapids: Zondervan, 2002), 86.

[31] Winebrenner, *Intimate Faith*, 116.

"In solitude, we meet God. In solitude we leave behind our many activities, concerns, plans and projects, opinions and convictions, and enter into the presence of our loving God, naked, vulnerable, open and receptive. And there we see that He alone is God, that He alone is care, that He alone is forgiveness." [32] *— Henri Nouwen*

- Spend some time in solitude this week. Make it a point to draw away from people, turn off the TV, the radio, the computer, your smartphone, and just spend some time alone with God. Nothing else. No one else.

---

[32] Henri Nouwen, *Modern Spirituality Series* (Springfield, IL: Templegate Publishers, 1988), 77.

DAY 2: THE DISCIPLINE OF SILENCE

Yesterday we looked at the discipline of solitude. Solitude and silence often go together. But we can be in solitude and still not be in silence. We may pray, but if we're doing all the talking, we are not able to listen to what God wants to say to us. Or if we surround ourselves with noise (TV, radio, music, etc.), we are not experiencing silence. Today we're going to focus on the discipline of silence and how it goes hand in hand with solitude in helping us rest.

LOOKING TO GOD'S WORD

1. As you read Psalm 62:1–2, 5–6, write down what you learn about silence. When should we observe it? Why? What can result from it?

2. Read Psalm 65. Be silent before Him. What attributes of God does David emphasize? Meditate on them as you sit before Him in silence.

LOOKING UPWARD

3. How do stillness and silence before God enlarge our understanding of who He is?

4. What hinders you from times of silence? What can you change in order to have more times of silence?

5. What are the dangers of constant noise around us?

LOOKING REFLECTIVELY

"I think the devil has made it his business to monopolize on three elements: noise, hurry, crowds ... Satan is quite aware of the power of silence." [33] —Jim Elliott

"The discipline of silence ... asks me: Do I have to have control and credit, or can I be silent and trust God to take control and handle this matter with His sovereign grace and power? It asks: Do I have to be the one who always has the last word, or am I content to let God have it?"[34]

- Pull away this week for some time in silence and solitude.

- While you're driving in your car, turn off the radio and phone. Just spend that time in silence. I have started doing that and loving that time free of "noise."

- As you spend time alone with God today, take five minutes to be silent. Don't ask for anything. Just be silent in His presence.

---

[33] John Blanchard, comp., *More Gathered Gold* (Welwyn, Hertfordshire, England: Evangelical Press, 1986), 295.

[34] Winebrenner, *Intimate Faith*, 126.

DAY 3: THE DISCIPLINE OF LISTENING

Taking time to be alone and silent enables us to hear God. Oftentimes, the world's noisiness drowns out what God is trying to tell us. Today we are going to look at the discipline of listening and how these three disciplines (solitude, silence, and listening) go together to bring us to a place of quiet rest.

LOOKING TO GOD'S WORD

1. Instead of looking at several passages and answering questions today, we're going to practice the discipline of listening by focusing on one passage. **Get alone. Turn off the noise around you**, and read Philippians 4:4–9. **Listen.** Meditate on this passage. Write out your thoughts. Ask God to speak to you through His Word. Listen. Be quiet. What does He want you to know as a result of this passage? What does He want you to do? You may want to write out the passage and make notes as you do. Put into practice the disciplines of solitude, silence, and listening.

LOOKING UPWARD

2. How does being alone enable you to listen to God?

3. Do you think it is always necessary to be totally isolated in order to hear God's voice? Explain your answer.

4. What is one thing God impressed on your heart from the passage today?

LOOKING REFLECTIVELY

"I am desperately concerned that we slow down so that each week we carve out time for quietness, solitude, thought, prayer, meditation, and soul-searching. Oh, how much agitation will begin to fade away; how insignificant petty differences will seem, how big God will become and how small our troubles will seem. Security, peace, and confidence will move right in." [35] — Chuck Swindoll

- Begin to incorporate these three disciplines into your life — solitude, silence, and listening. Which do you struggle with the most and why? Ask God to show you what you need to change to begin practicing these disciplines more faithfully.

---

[35] Charles R. Swindoll, *The Living Insights Study Bible, New International Version* (Grand Rapids, MI: Zondervan Publishing, 1996), 575.

DAY 4: THE DISCIPLINE OF MEDITATION

Many of us have reading plans to help us read through the Bible in a year. Those are good, but how much do we meditate on what we're reading? Are we just skimming the surface? It's important to read the Bible, and it's important to pray. But as Donald Whitney writes, "Meditation is the missing link between Bible intake and prayer. The two are often disjointed when they should be united. We read the Bible, close it, and then try to shift gears into prayer....

Instead there should be a smooth, almost unnoticeable transition between Scripture input and prayer output so that we move even closer to God in those moments. This happens when there is the link of meditation in between."[36]

Today we're going to practice the discipline of meditation.

LOOKING TO GOD'S WORD

1. Read through Psalm 19:7–14. List all the terms that David used for God's Word.

2. What is true of God's Word and what does it do for us?

3. Take the words David used to describe God's Word and meditate on each term.
   For example, God's Word is perfect. What does that mean? What are the implications for me? What difference does it make?

---

[36] Whitney, *Spiritual Disciplines for the Christian Life*, 67.

4. Now take each of the phrases David used to describe how the Word impacts us and meditate on each one.

   For example, it restores the soul. What does that mean? How does it restore my soul?

LOOKING UPWARD

5. Do you spend more time meditating on God's Word or just reading God's Word?

6. What hinders you from meditating on God's Word?

LOOKING REFLECTIVELY

Spend time in prayer reflecting on the passage today. Ask God to use His Word in your life as described in these verses. Personalize these words to your life.

DAY 5: THE DISCIPLINE OF SIMPLICITY

When we're busy and distracted by all the to-dos on our lists, we find it hard to rest. Our minds race, adrenaline kicks in to help us move faster and plan out how we're going to get everything done. We are tempted by the material possessions of this world, and we want more. So we work harder. And the more we have, the more time it takes to maintain what we have. We need rest, but it seems to escape us.

This week we've looked at several spiritual disciplines that can help us slow down and find rest as we meet with God. Today we conclude our look at spiritual disciplines by focusing on the discipline of simplicity. When we take our eyes off earthly things and tasks to be done and focus on the One who is in control of everything happening around us, we will find rest.

LOOKING TO GOD'S WORD

1. Jesus spoke often about wealth and material possessions. As you read Matthew 6:19–21, list the commands that Jesus gave.

2. What are some of the reasons for following these commands?

3. In Matthew 6:21, Jesus states, "For where your treasure is, there your heart will be also." What is your treasure? How does it affect your ability or inability to rest?

4. As you continue reading Matthew 6:25–34, what phrase does Jesus repeat throughout this passage?

5. What is Jesus emphasizing in this passage? What does He want them to do and not do?

LOOKING UPWARD

6. What is the solution to worry?

7. How does this passage relate to the discipline of simplicity? And how does this passage lead us to rest?

LOOKING REFLECTIVELY

"We simplify, not just to be less busy, even though we may be right to pursue that. Rather, we simplify to remove distractions from our pursuit of Christ. We prune activities from our lives, not only to get organized, but also that our devotion to Christ and service for His kingdom will be more fruitful. We simplify, not merely to save time, but to eliminate hindrances to the time we devote to knowing Christ. All the reasons we simplify should eventually lead us to Jesus Christ." [37]—Donald Whitney

- What things are distracting you from your pursuit of Christ?

---

[37] Donald Whitney, *Simplify Your Spiritual Life* (Colorado Springs: NavPress, 2003), 26.

Cynthia Heald writes in her Bible study, *Becoming a Woman of Simplicity*:

> *"My concern is that we live in a world where doing, communicating, and possessing so rule our lives that we have allowed even good things to overtake our time and distract from the best.... My definition of a woman of simplicity is one who lives a God-paced life. She waits for God's leading, and she has time to be still and know her Lord. She has a deep abiding rest in her spirit. She is a woman of profound simplicity because she has only one focus: being simply and purely devoted to Christ."*[38]

- Ask God to show you one thing you can do to simplify your life.

- Memorize and meditate on 2 Corinthians 11:3.

---

[38] Cynthia Heald, *Becoming a Woman of Simplicity* (Colorado Springs: NavPress, 2009), 15.

WEEK 8

THE PROMISE OF REST

As we conclude our study of rest this week, it would not be complete without looking at these final passages. I pray that, as a result of this study, you have a better picture of what biblical rest is and that you would fully embrace His rest.

DAY 1: CANAAN REST (Part 1)

For most of this week, we will be looking at Hebrews 3:7–4:11. One of my professors in seminary, Dr. Stanley Toussaint, suggested there are three rests being described in Hebrews 3 and 4. Today and tomorrow, we are going to focus on the first rest, Canaan rest. This is the rest that God promised Israel upon entering the Promised Land under Joshua.

LOOKING TO GOD'S WORD

Hebrews 3:7–11; Psalm 95

1. In Hebrews 3:7–11, the author of Hebrews refers back to Psalm 95, warning these Jewish believers to not follow the example of the Israelites. Read Psalm 95. Mark each time David uses the words "come" and "let us." What is he asking his readers to come and do?

2. As you look at David's warnings to the readers in Psalm 95:7–11, what did he exhort them to do or not do?

3. Looking at both Psalm 95:7–11 and Hebrews 3:7–11, what did the Israelites do? How did God respond to them? (Compare the two passages.)

    Psalm 95   Hebrews 3

LOOKING DEEPER (Optional)

This quotation in Hebrews 3:7–11 refers back to two Old Testament events. The specific places are recorded in Psalm 95. According to the following verses, where and what were these two events? What happened at each place?

   1st event—Exodus 17:1–7

   2nd event—Numbers 14:1–38

LOOKING UPWARD

4. How would you recognize a hardened heart in yourself or someone else?

5. In what ways do we provoke God today? Can you give a specific example?

LOOKING REFLECTIVELY

Spend some time praising God, using Psalm 95 as a guide.

- Are you testing God or provoking Him in any way? If so, confess it.

DAY 2: CANAAN REST (Part 2)

Today we continue our look at Canaan rest as the author of Hebrews warns and admonishes his readers not to follow the example of the Israelites who provoked God.

LOOKING TO GOD'S WORD

Hebrews 3:12–19

1. In Hebrews 3:12–15, what are the dangers the author warns against? What exhortations does he give?

2. In 3:16–18, the author asks a series of questions. Write the question and to whom he was referring with each question.

3. Describe God's response to their behavior.

4. What prevented them from entering God's rest in Canaan (3:18–19)?

5. Some have interpreted verses 12–14 to mean that you can fall away from God and lose your salvation. But Scripture does not support that view (John 10:27–30; Ephesians 1:13; 1 John 5:11–13). What do you think the author means in Hebrews 3:12–14?

LOOKING UPWARD

6. What would it look like to encourage one another day after day in order to prevent becoming "hardened by the deceitfulness of sin" (3:13)?

7. In what ways are we deceived by sin and how does it lead to a hardened heart?

LOOKING REFLECTIVELY

The author of Hebrews was warning these readers to not make the same mistake their ancestors made. Their ancestors did not enter God's rest, the Promised Land, because they didn't believe God. They failed to possess their inheritance because they didn't trust God, they disobeyed God, and they hardened their hearts. Only Joshua and Caleb entered the Promised Land because they followed God fully. (For more on this, read Numbers 14:21–24, 30.)

- Are you in danger of allowing the deceitfulness of sin to harden your heart? If so, what do you need to do in order to prevent that from happening?

Is there someone you can encourage to rest in the Lord today, instead of falling into the deceitfulness of sin? What is one thing you can do this week to encourage that person?

Do you need to rest in the Lord today?

DAY 3: THE PROMISED REST

In Hebrews 3, the author referred back to the Canaan rest. The Israelites didn't experience this rest because of their disbelief and disobedience to God when they received the negative reports from those who spied out the land. So they wandered in the wilderness for forty years until that generation of adults died.

The Jewish Christians to whom the letter of Hebrews was addressed were in danger of following in the footsteps of their ancestors. They were tempted to doubt the words of Jesus and go back to Judaism. Today we will focus on the second rest described — the promised rest. In Hebrews 4, the author of Hebrews explains what this rest is and shows why it is available to us today.

LOOKING TO GOD'S WORD

Hebrews 4:1–11

1. What two exhortations does the author give his readers in verses 1 and 11? (Look for the phrase "let us.")

2. How would someone come short of entering His rest (4:2)?

> **Note:** In verse 2, the "good news preached to us" (NASB95) is the translation from a single Greek word meaning "the good news was announced." The good news of God's rest had been proclaimed to the Israelites. The generation led by Moses had failed to enter their rest (the Promised Land, Deut. 12:9) because of their lack of faith. In the same way, the gospel of Christ that had been proclaimed to the audience of this letter was calling them into

God's rest, but their unbelief would hinder them from entering into it.[39]

3. How does someone today enter God's rest (4:2–3)?

4. Why is the promise of God's rest still valid today according to this passage?

5. What do you think is the significance of the author's reference to God's rest at creation? What is the connection to the rest he is talking about here?

LOOKING UPWARD

6. Do you think he's referring to the promised rest as present rest (rest of conscience because believers know their sins are forgiven) or future rest (that final rest in glory) or both? Why?

LOOKING REFLECTIVELY

From the time of Creation, God has been offering rest to us. But will we enter into that rest? Or will we miss out like some of the Israelites because of disobedience, lack of faith, or a hardened heart? Ask God to reveal to you areas that might be hindering you from fully embracing His rest.

- What do you learn about God from today's passage?

---

39 Earl Radmacher, Ronald B. Allen, and H. Wayne House, *Nelson's New Illustrated Bible Commentary* (Nashville: Thomas Nelson, 1999), 1641.

DAY 4: THE SABBATH REST

So far, we have looked at two kinds of rest: Canaan rest in Hebrews 3, and the promised rest in Hebrews 4. Today we look at a third rest, found in Hebrews 4—Sabbath rest.

LOOKING TO GOD'S WORD

Hebrews 4:9–11

1. Read Hebrews 4:1–11 again and mark each occurrence of the word **rest**. Also mark the occurrence of this word in Hebrews 3:11–18.

> **Note:** The Greek word for *rest* in Hebrews 4:9 is different from the word used in the other verses. This word means "Sabbath rest" and is found only here in the New Testament.[40]

2. What do you think the author means by *Sabbath rest* in Hebrews 4:9? How do the following verses give insight to the meaning of *Sabbath rest* here?

    Hebrews 4:4, 10

    Genesis 2:2–3

    Exodus 20:11

---

[40] Radmacher, Allen, and House, *Nelson New Illustrated Bible Commentary*, 1641.

3. How does Sabbath rest differ from Canaan rest and the promised rest, or does it?

4. What do you think he means by "his works" in Hebrews 4:10?

5. Verse 10 has been interpreted as having a present application, a future application, or both. What is your interpretation and why? Can you support your interpretation with Scripture?

LOOKING UPWARD

6. Do you think *Sabbath rest* means rest on a specific day of the week or just taking time to rest on a regular basis to be replenished and refreshed? Explain your answer.

LOOKING REFLECTIVELY

• Read Hebrews 4:12–16. What do you learn about God's Word?

• What do you learn about Jesus?

• Spend some time thanking God for His Word and for Jesus as our High Priest. Meditate on these verses.

DAY 5: THE PLACE OF REST

As we conclude our study of rest today, we will look at a familiar and well-loved passage—Matthew 11:28–30. But to understand what Jesus means in these verses, we must first look at the context and the audience to whom He was speaking. He was addressing the people of Israel who were burdened and weighed down with the legal dos and don'ts of the Pharisees, and with the consequences—the guilt, frustration, and dissatisfaction that always goes along with legalism. They were weary trying to keep the laws, trying to earn salvation through their own good works. Jesus wanted to set them free from this oppressive burden, and He wants to set us free. He invited them and He invites us to come to Him for rest. Stop trying; stop striving; rest in Jesus. He has done all that is necessary for our salvation. Go to Him and find rest.

LOOKING TO GOD'S WORD

Matthew 11:28–30

1. Jesus extends the invitation to rest to the weary and heavy-laden. How does one become weary and heavy-laden?

2. What does Jesus ask them to do? What are the three commands? What do you think each command means?

3. What does Jesus promise if they follow these instructions?

4. To what type of rest do you think He is referring (salvation rest, present rest found in Him, or future rest in glory)? Explain your answer.

5. There were also believers in the audience who had already come to Christ. What does "come to Me" mean for believers?

LOOKING UPWARD

6. Jesus told them to take His yoke upon them. For nonbelievers, what does that mean and how would that lead to rest?

7. For believers, this was an invitation to discipleship; to wholeheartedly follow Jesus, yielding to His lordship in their lives. How would that lead to rest?

LOOKING REFLECTIVELY

"To all of us Christ offers 'rest,' not in the other life only, but in this. Rest from the weight of sin, from care and worry, from the load of daily anxiety and foreboding. The rest that arrives from handing all worries over to Christ and receiving from Christ all we need. Have we entered into that experience?" [41]—F.B. Myer

Jesus Christ offers us rest. Reflect on the passages below and thank Him for the rest we can enjoy today in the present and in the future eternally.

*   **Salvation rest**—rest from having to work for our salvation

    Ephesians 1:13–14

    Ephesians 2:8–9

---

[41] Bruce Barton, Dave Veerman, and Linda Taylor, *Life Application Bible Commentary: Hebrews* (Carol Stream, IL: Tyndale, 1997), 49.

- **Eternal rest—**

  Revelation 14:13

  Revelation 21:1–4

From *The Valley of Vision*:

Most Holy God,

May the close of an earthly Sabbath remind me that the last of them will one day end. Animate me with joy that in heaven praise will never cease, that adoration will continue forever, that no flesh will grow weary, no congregations disperse, no affections flag, no thoughts wander ... but all will be adoring love.

Guard my mind from making ordinances my stay or trust, from hewing out broken cisterns, from resting on outward helps. Wing me through earthly forms to Thy immediate presence; May my feeble prayers show me the emptiness and vanity of my sins;

Deepen in me the conviction that my most fervent prayers, and most lowly confessions, need to be repented of. May my best services bring me nearer to the cross and prompt me to cry, "None but Jesus!"

By Thy Spirit give abiding life to the lessons of this day: may the seed sown take deep root and yield a full harvest.

Let all who see me take knowledge that I have been with Thee, that Thou hast taught me my need as a sinner, hast revealed a finished salvation to me, hast enriched me with all spiritual blessings, hast chosen me to show forth Jesus to others, hast helped me dispel the mists of unbelief.

O great Creator, mighty Protector, gracious Preserver, Thou dost load me with loving kindnesses, and hast made me Thy purchased possession, and redeemed me from all guilt;

I praise and bless Thee for my Sabbath rest, my calm conscience, my peace of heart. [42]

Lord, help us embrace the gift of rest.

---

[42] Arthur Bennett, *The Valley of Vision: A Collection of Puritan Prayers and Devotions* (Carlisle, PA: The Banner of Truth Trust, 1975), 364–365.

BIBLIOGRAPHY

Allender, Dan. *Sabbath: The Ancient Practices*. Nashville: Thomas Nelson, 2009.

Barton, Bruce and Philip Comfort, et al. *Life Application New Testament Commentary*. Wheaton: Tyndale, 2001.

Barton, Bruce and Dave Veerman and Linda Taylor. *Life Application Bible Commentary: Hebrews*. Carol Stream, IL: Tyndale, 1997.

Bennett, Arthur. *The Valley of Vision: A Collection of Puritan Prayers and Devotions*. Carlisle, PA: The Banner of Truth Trust, 1975.

Blanchard, John. *More Gathered Gold*. Welwyn, Hertfordshire, England: Evangelical Press, 1986.

Buchanan, Mark. *The Gift of Rest*. Nashville: Thomas Nelson, 2006.

Carmichael, Amy. *Edges of His Ways*. Fort Washington, PA: Christian Literature Crusade, 1989.

Chambers, Oswald. *My Utmost for His Highest, An Updated Edition in Today's Language*. Grand Rapids: Discovery House, 2010.

Deffinbaugh,Bob. *The Meaning of the Sabbath*. http://bible.org/seriespage/meaning-sabbath-exodus-208-11, Accessed 5/10/2013.

Feinberg, Margaret. *Resting in Him: I Need to Slow Down but I Can't!* Nashville: Thomas Nelson, 2008.

George, Denise. *A Woman's Right to Rest.* Abilene, TX: Leafwood, 2012.

Heald, Cynthia. *Becoming a Woman of Simplicity.* Colorado Springs: NavPress, 2009.

Hummel, Charles E. *Tyranny of the Urgent.* Madison, WI: InterVarsity Christian Fellowship, 1967.

Hybels, Bill. *Honest to God? Becoming an Authentic Christian.* Grand Rapids: Zondervan, 1990.

Keller, Phillip. *A Shepherd Looks at Psalm 23.* Grand Rapids: Zondervan, 1970.

Knowles, Andrew. *The Bible Guide.* Minneapolis: Augsburg, 2001.

MacArthur, John. *The Rest of Creation,* Genesis 2:1-3. August 29, 1999. http://www.gty.org/Resources/Sermons/90-221, Accessed July 24, 2013.

MacDonald, William. *Believer's Bible Commentary: Old and New Testaments.* Nashville: Thomas Nelson, 1995.

Murray, Andrew. *Waiting on God.* New Kensington, PA: Whitaker House, 1983.

Nouwen, Henri. *Modern Spirituality Series.* Springfield, IL: Templegate, 1988.

Ortberg, John. *The Life You've Always Wanted.* Grand Rapids: Zondervan, 2002.

Radmacher, Earl, Ron B. Allen, and H. Wayne House. *Nelson's New Illustrated Bible Commentary.* Nashville: Thomas Nelson Publishers, 1999.

Richards, L. and L.O. Richards. *The Teacher's Commentary.* Wheaton: Victor Books, 1987.

Swindoll, Charles R. *The Living Insights Study Bible, New International Version*. Grand Rapids: Zondervan, 1996.

Whitney, Donald. *Simplify Your Spiritual Life*. Colorado Springs: NavPress, 2003.

_____. *Spiritual Disciplines for the Christian Life*. Colorado Springs: NavPress, 1991.

Wiersbe, Warren. *The Bible Exposition Commentary: Pentateuch*. Colorado Springs: Victor Books, 2001.

_____. *Be Comforted*. Wheaton: Victor Books, 1996.

_____. *Meet Yourself in the Psalms*. Wheaton: Victor Books, 1986.

Winebrenner, Jan. *Intimate Faith: A Woman's Guide to the Spiritual Disciplines*. New York: Warner Books, 2003.